BRAY WYATT
BIOGRAPHY

**A Twisted Tale of Triumph and Darkness of
The Mind Games Master and His Tragic
Demise.**

James E. Clark

Table of Contents

Introduction

A run-through of Bray Wyatt's life

Windham's early life was shaped by the legacy of his wrestling family, and his eventual transformation into Bray Wyatt redefined the boundaries of storytelling in sports entertainment.

On the 23rd of May, 1987, Windham Lawrence Rotunda was born in the small town of Brooksville, Florida. Little did anyone know that this birth would mark the beginning of the world of professional wrestling.

Windham was a third-generation wrestler, following in the footsteps of his grandfather Blackjack Mulligan, his father Mike Rotunda, and two of his uncles – Barry and Kendall Windham. His younger brother Taylor Rotunda is also a professional wrestler, known as Bo Dallas.

Windham was an American professional wrestler and a high school state champion amateur wrestler and college football player in his youth. He first wrestled in WWE from 2009 to 2011 under the name Husky Harris and was a part of the stable, The Nexus.

He competed on the 2nd season of WWE NXT and stayed in WWE's developmental territory, Florida Championship Wrestling (FCW). In April 2012, he made his debut as Bray Wyatt in FCW and returned to the main WWE roster in July 2013.

Alongside his brother, he held the FCW Florida Tag Team Championship twice. He also became a three-time world champion in WWE, holding the WWE Championship once and the Universal Championship twice. He also held the SmackDown Tag Team Championship (with Luke Harper and Randy Orton under the

Freebird Rule) and the Raw Tag Team Championship (with Matt Hardy) once each.

In August 2018, he took a hiatus from WWE and returned in April 2019 with a new gimmick. He was portrayed as suffering from a transformative multiple personality disorder, switching back and forth between two characters: his "good side" of Bray Wyatt, a Mr. Rogers–esque children's TV host, and his bad side of The Fiend, a grotesque horror-themed monster clown.

He was released from WWE in July 2021 but returned to Extreme Rules in October 2022, with a new character that claimed to be his "real-life" self but gradually re-incorporated his multiple personalities in addition to some new ones.

Chapter One

Wrestling in His Blood: A Wyatt Family Legacy

The Rotunda family has left an indelible mark in the world of sports entertainment. Windham Rotunda was surrounded by the larger-than-life tales of his grandfather, Blackjack Mulligan, and his father, Mike Rotunda (known to wrestling fans as Irwin R. Schyster or IRS).

This passion for wrestling was passed down to Windham, who absorbed the spectacle and theatrics of the sport like a sponge. His brothers, Taylor and Bo, also went on to make their marks in professional wrestling, further solidifying the Rotunda family's legacy.

Windham had the physical prowess, charisma, and storytelling ability to make his mark in the world of wrestling. He was more than just a reflection of his family's past; he was a harbinger of the future, a future that would be shrouded in darkness and intrigue, a future that would become synonymous with the name Bray Wyatt.

The Early Years: Finding His Path

He attended Hernando High School, where he won a state wrestling championship at 275 pounds (125 kg) in 2005, the year of his graduation. He also played football as a defensive tackle and guard. Rotunda played at the College of the Sequoias for two seasons, earning second-team All-American honors as a sophomore offensive guard at the California junior college.

He earned a football scholarship to Troy University, where he played college football for two years. He left Troy 27 credit hours short of earning a bachelor's degree after deciding to pursue a career in professional wrestling.

Windham's fascination with wrestling began as he watched his father, Mike Rotunda, in action as Irwin R. Schyster (IRS) in WWE. The television screen became a portal to a world of larger-than-life characters and epic battles, igniting a spark within the young boy. He was drawn to the spectacle and the adrenaline of professional wrestling.

As Windham navigated his early years, he faced the challenge of living up to the legacy of the Rotunda name while also forging his own identity. It was a delicate balancing act, one that would shape his evolution from a wrestling prodigy to the mastermind behind Bray Wyatt and the "Firefly Fun House."

Chapter Two

The Transformation: Breaking Free From Husky Harris to Bray Wyatt

Since joining fellow Wyatt Family members Luke Harper and Erick Rowan on the main roster in 2013, Bray Wyatt has been one of the most prominent Superstars on WWE programming.

Before that, he wrestled for Florida Championship Wrestling's developmental program between 2010 and 2012 as a character named Husky Harris. However, his main roster run lasted only a few months before he returned.

It was obvious from the start of the re-debut of the repackaged Bray Wyatt that he was going to succeed despite his nasty antics and fascinating character as a cult leader.

The Birth of a New Persona: The Eater of Worlds

Due to his former cult leader persona, Bray Wyatt is known as The Eater of Worlds. The persona consistently outran and defeated his opponents while claiming to be God. As a result of his godlike nature and extraordinary skills, he was given the nickname "The Eater of Worlds."

Who gave Bray Wyatt the nickname "Eater of Worlds"?
One of the wrestling industry's brightest minds is Bray Wyatt. Fans loved his time as The Eater of Worlds; they joined him as his firefly and responded favorably to him each week. The term, nevertheless, wasn't created by the previous world champion. Wyatt's name was created by WWE Hall of Famer Dusty Rhodes.

Due to his character's otherworldliness, Rhodes dubbed him "The Eater of Worlds."

It gave his gimmick an added edge and was the ideal fit for it. The term does fit him to a tee, as evidenced by one of his innumerable cryptic promos: "You think you need someone to tuck you in at night, kiss you on the cheek, and reassure you that everything is okay. However, NOTHING IS RIGHT WITH EVERYTHING... EVERYTHING... EVERYTHING! How would you react if I revealed that the person who created you is a liar? What if I told you that your blood relative had abandoned you? Never would I turn away from you. And perhaps, just perhaps, the solutions you seek have been staring you in the face. Or perhaps I, Bray Wyatt, the Eater of Worlds, am the solution after all.

Crafting the Character

Bray Wyatt has a special talent for persuading people to buy into the mystique and allure of professional wrestling. Your attention was immediately captured when Bray Wyatt said, "We're here."

Wyatt would stroll out with a lantern in hand as The Wyatt Family approached, followed by an eerie-faced Luke Harper and a sheep mask-wearing Erick Rowan. In comparison to those two giants, Wyatt appeared to be of average size. But Wyatt created a figure that was full of deceit; as we quickly discovered, the man was anything but typical.

Chapter Three

Gaining Notoriety

The debut of NXT-The Cult Leader Emerges

Rotunda was rebranded as Bray Wyatt in April 2012; he had previously identified with Eli Cottonwood in FCW. Bray Wyatt was sent to NXT to reinvent himself when WWE renamed FCW as NXT Wrestling. He made a big impression right away, taking on the character of a cult leader and making an appearance with his followers even on the episode of the revived NXT that was filmed at Full Sail University and included Aiden English being defeated.

Wyatt soon rose to prominence as one of the most well-liked wrestlers in NXT thanks to his ominous and sinister promos. In 2014, he captured the NXT Championship, which he held for more than a year.

The Wyatt Family: A Reign of Terror

In the WWE, Bray Wyatt's ascent to fame was swift. Luke Harper and Erick Rowan were among the followers he swiftly gathered, and the three of them later came to be known as The Wyatt Family.

The Wyatt Family swiftly rose to prominence in the WWE as one of its most feared and admired factions. Their matches were frequently violent and chaotic, and they were noted for their ominous and gloomy personalities. Bray Wyatt was an expert at mind tricks and frequently exploited his adversaries' anxieties.

The Wyatt Family ruled with terror for several years. They terrified John Cena, Randy Orton, and Daniel Bryan, three of the biggest names in the WWE. They twice even took home the WWE Tag Team Championships.

But everything nice has to come to an end. In the end, The Wyatt Family split up in 2017. After that, Bray Wyatt enjoyed success in the singles game and twice claimed the WWE Championship. Both as solo wrestlers and as a tag team, Luke Harper and Erick Rowan went on to enjoy prosperous professional wrestling careers.

Despite the death of the Wyatt family, their legacy endures. One of the most distinctive and enduring groups in WWE history, their influence on the organization is still felt today.

Fighting with the Biggest Names: The Shield, John Cena, and More

When Bray Wyatt decided to take on John Cena, the leader of the Cenation, it was one of his most pivotal moments. The WWE Universe had become accustomed to seeing Cena as the unflappable hero, but Wyatt's unsettling presence called into question Cena's very persona. Their conflict was a psychological mind game as much as a contest of skills.

Fans saw a change in Cena like never before as Bray Wyatt exploited his sense of morality and drove him to his limit. Cena knew he couldn't outmuscle the face of terror by using just raw force. This conflict served as a turning point in Bray Wyatt's career, proving him to be a skilled storyteller with the ability to sway the opinions of even the most steadfast heroes.

Roman Reigns, Seth Rollins, and Dean Ambrose made up the powerful three known in the WWE as "The Shield," who were renowned for their cohesion and dominance. On the other hand, Bray Wyatt was a lone evil force. The WWE Universe was in for a rollercoaster of pandemonium when these two forces came together.

Intense clashes between Wyatt and The Shield demonstrated Bray's cleverness and his capacity for using mind tricks to split and subdue his opponents. Some of the most cherished moments in WWE history were produced by these clashes, which brought out the best in both groups. Fans were on the edge of their seats as a layer of mystery was added to the conflict by Bray Wyatt's spooky charisma and cryptic promos.

Chapter Four

The Character's Backstory: The Mind of Bray Wyatt

Creating His Promos

Making the advertisements for Bray Wyatt is no simple chore. Bray is the mastermind planning these grotesque shows behind the scenes.

The promotional material for Bray Wyatt is psychological warfare, not simply words. Bray Wyatt's promos are an essential part of creating his persona and feuds, from his cryptic words to the creepy presence of the Firefly Fun House. They leave followers speculating, making assumptions, and eagerly awaiting their next move.

The Family Dynamic: Luke Harper, Erick Rowan

The Wyatt Family was a tag team in professional wrestling who belonged to the cult faction.

Luke Harper and Erick Rowan worked at house shows from June 2012 to November 2012, then in January 2013, they made their televised debut as a tag team.

In May 2013, they triumphed as a team to win the NXT Tag Team Championship. After The Wyatt Family broke up in late 2014, they were promoted to the main roster and soon began a feud with one another. In May 2015, they got back together, and they later made amends with Wyatt, reestablishing The Wyatt Family. Due to injuries sustained during the group's comeback, Harper and Rowan were inactive in 2016.

In October 2017, the pair got back together as a team under the new name The Bludgeon

Brothers, with their ring names abbreviated to Harper and Rowan. They ultimately won the SmackDown Tag Team Championship at WrestleMania 34 in April 2018. After losing the belts that August, they were separated due to injuries for some time until coming back together in September 2019 and ditching the Bludgeon Brothers persona in favor of their previous ring identities.

That was their final time working together, though, as Rowan was selected for Raw during the 2019 WWE draft while Harper stayed on SmackDown. Rowan was subsequently released in April 2020 as a result of financial cuts brought on by the COVID-19 pandemic, while Harper was subsequently dropped from the promotion in December due to artistic differences.

Following their respective releases from WWE, Rowan started wrestling on the independent scene as Erick Redbeard while Harper joined All Elite Wrestling (AEW) under the ring name Brodie Lee.

Harper passed away suddenly on December 26, 2020; on December 30, during an AEW memorial show, Rowan made his debut in the promotion and paid tribute to his late tag team partner by holding up a sign in the ring that said, "Goodbye for now, my brother. I'll see you later on.

The Firefly Fun House: A Look Into Bray's Psyche

There was a whimsical and puzzling aspect of Bray Wyatt's persona known as the Firefly Fun House that existed amid the mayhem and darkness of his wrestling career.

The Firefly Fun House was unheard of in the history of wrestling. It was a children's television show, hosted by Bray Wyatt, with bright puppets, catchy jingles, and an ambiance that seemed innocent. However, the darkness that characterized Bray's personality was hidden beneath this appearance of purity.

The Fun House served as a simile for Bray's psychological breakdown. From the amiable Rambling Rabbit to the unsettling Mercy the Buzzard, each figure in the play represented various facets of Bray's character and history. With the help of these puppet personalities, Bray seemed to be battling his inner demons.

The Fiend was arguably the most recognizable and disturbing character in the Fun House. This horrifying alter ego represented Bray's darkest instincts. The conflict between Bray Wyatt's evil and his desire to amuse people was highlighted by his dual identity as The Fiend, which gave his character more complexity.

The Place of The Fiend in Wrestling History
One of the most distinctive and well-liked characters in the annals of professional wrestling is The Fiend. He is a twisted, demonic being that represents Bray Wyatt's inner depravity. The

WWE's The Fiend is one of the most talked-about personas, despite being a divisive personality.

The Fiend made his WWE debut in 2019, and he rapidly rose to fame as one of the company's most well-known characters. He has some of the most cherished matches in WWE history and twice won the Universal Championship.

The figure known as The Fiend defies accepted wrestling conventions. He does not fit the mold of a typical "face" or "heel." He is a natural force and is not constrained by the same laws as other wrestlers.

A surge in interest in wrestling characters with a horror theme has emerged as a result of The Fiend's success. Other wrestlers have adapted aspects of The Fiend's persona, like his use of mind tricks and slow, methodical pace, like Malakai Black in AEW.

Each week, as viewers turned in, they were treated to a mix of outrageous humor and spooky scenes that merged reality and fantasy. The Firefly Fun House episodes left viewers both curious and bewildered since they were thought-provoking as well as enjoyable.

The Firefly Fun House wasn't just a place to have fun; it also allowed Bray Wyatt to make deeper points. His advertisements frequently featured messages like accepting oneself, embracing one's inner darkness, and the notion that everyone hides their actual selves behind masks. Fans connected with these concepts deeply, making Bray's character one of the most fascinating in contemporary wrestling.

Chapter Five

The WrestleMania Moments

Bray Wyatt has painted some of his most memorable moments on WrestleMania, the largest stage in the WWE.

Taking on John Cena in the Steel Cage at WrestleMania 30

Bray Wyatt's career was changed forever at WrestleMania 30 as he entered the biggest stage of them all to compete against wrestling legend John Cena. The match was a confrontation of philosophies, characters, and generations, taking place inside the harsh confines of a steel cage.

With a past that gave the rivalry more layers of complexity, the stage was prepared for this dramatic confrontation. Bray Wyatt had been pursuing John Cena for months with his uncanny charisma and mysterious words. He challenged Cena's image as a paragon of virtue and morals to reveal what he saw as Cena's deeper, more sinister sides.

Bray Wyatt and his supporters, the Wyatt Family, waged psychological combat in the run-up to WrestleMania. To enter John Cena's psyche, they employed unpleasant mental tricks. This included unsettling advertisements, unsettling graphics, and even a children's choir singing "He's Got the Whole World in His Hands," which helped to establish the mood for the fight.

Making this a Steel Cage match was a huge choice. Their competition became even more intense as a result of being confined inside the cage and being protected from outside intervention. Cena would be unable to leave the cage, and it would be a test of both his physical and mental toughness.

At WrestleMania 30, the tension was audible as the bell rang. Cena's more conventional approach clashed with Bray Wyatt's unconventional wrestling style. They used the cage as a weapon, pushing each other into the harsh steel mesh, and the steel structure provided an element of danger.

This contest was exceptional because of the psychological component. The mental tricks of Bray Wyatt persisted inside the cage. He frequently teased and irritated Cena, driving him to the brink. In addition to wrestling prowess, mental toughness and resilience were also tested.

In the end, Bray Wyatt triumphed, pinning John Cena during a hard contest. For Bray, this victory was a critical turning point in his career and cemented his place as a powerful force in the WWE. Because Cena was forced to face his demons throughout the feud, it also added a fascinating chapter to his career.

WrestleMania 33: The House of Horrors Match with Randy Orton

The House of Horrors Match between Bray Wyatt and Randy Orton at WrestleMania 33 will always be remembered in the annals of WrestleMania history. This unusual and unnerving meeting took occurred outside the typical WrestleMania venue, giving the biggest stage of them all a bizarre and nightmare dimension.

With Wyatt's sinister mind tricks and Orton's resolve to reveal the mystery that was Bray, the tension had been building for months. The contest was expected to feature both physical and mental adversity.

This match's venue was what made it genuinely exceptional. The House of Horrors was a dark, abandoned house that appeared to be haunted. The anxiety was increased by the ominous sounds and frightening pictures that added to the ominous and unpleasant atmosphere.

The Haunted House Match started within the mansion, with both participants fighting their way through its unsettling hallways and coming across terrible scenes. This includes doll-filled rooms, a mysterious gift in the refrigerator, and even paranormal contact with Bray Wyatt's insane mind.

After the match's house segment, the action returned to the WrestleMania arena, where Randy Orton and Bray Wyatt continued to wrestle. Orton surprised everyone by winning the bout, but the psychological scars from the House of Horrors persisted long after the final buzzer.

Regardless of opinions, the battle was a divisive spectacle that demonstrated Bray Wyatt's determination to push the limits of sports entertainment and produce scenes that were more akin to horror films than wrestling matches.

WrestleMania 36: The Bizarre Battle with John Cena

At WrestleMania 36, Bray Wyatt and John Cena engaged in a genuinely peculiar contest. Bray Wyatt, now known as "The Fiend," set out on a mission to confront John Cena because he saw him as the embodiment of all the injustices and setbacks in his professional life. Cena would have to confront his past and mistakes in this collision of the past and present.

The Fiend used his well-known psychological tricks in the run-up to WrestleMania 36. He played on Cena's anxieties and vulnerabilities. Their conflict gained complexity thanks to this psychological conflict, elevating it above the level of a simple wrestling battle.

It was described as a "Firefly Fun House Match," which muddled the distinction between the actual world and Bray Wyatt's warped existence. The match took place outside of the conventional wrestling ring and consisted of several fantastical and symbolic situations.

Each part of the Firefly Fun House Match represented a distinct period or aspect of John Cena's persona, taking viewers on a journey through his career. It covered topics including regret, lost chances, and the results of one's actions.

There were multiple allusions to Cena's and The Fiend's pasts, as well as callbacks to their prior confrontations, throughout the match.

The Fiend triumphed in the final battle, signifying the victory of evil. It was a complex and thought-provoking climax that astounded both the audience and the critics with its originality and breadth.

The Challenges of a WWE Career: Injuries and Setbacks

Bray Wyatt encountered many challenges throughout his WWE career that put his resiliency and resolve to the test.

Injury setbacks during Bray Wyatt's early years in the WWE prevented him from progressing. These setbacks frequently happened when he was gathering momentum, necessitating time away from the ring for recuperation.

Bray Wyatt's catastrophic ankle injury in 2016 was one of the most noticeable setbacks. He missed several months of in-ring competition as a result of this injury. He kept refining his character work and promos during this period, which kept the audience interested even when he wasn't present.

Another turn in Bray's career occurred when an intended plot featuring the "Sister Abigail" aspect of his character had to be changed because of unanticipated events.

The debut of the Firefly Fun House and "The Fiend" character marked perhaps the biggest comeback in Bray's career. His career was given fresh life by this imaginative rethinking, which also demonstrated his ability to change and grow in the face of obstacles.

Chapter 6

The Man Behind the Masks: Family life

The importance of Windham's family to him meant that they were more than simply a minor detail in his life story. Windham had a deep appreciation for the sacrifices his family made to help him pursue his dreams of becoming a wrestler throughout his entire life.

Sibling(s)

A real-life brother of Wyatt who competes in professional wrestling. By taking on the role of Bo Dallas in the WWE, Taylor Michael Rotunda rose to prominence in the wrestling community. From 2008 until 2021, he wrestled professionally for WWE. During that time, he won the WWE Raw Tag Team Championship, and the WWE 24/7 Championship, and briefly held the NXT Championship.

The relationship Windham had with his brother Taylor Rotunda was among the most important and endearing components of his family life. More than merely a source of mutual support, their sibling relationship gave them a sense of unity and strength.

Marriage

Windham was married, but the relationship did not end well. From 2012 to 2017, Bray Wyatt and Samantha Rotunda were wed. Samantha sought a divorce after the marriage broke down because she claimed Bray had cheated on her. Since her divorce, Samantha has remarried and works as a real estate agent for Southern Belle Realty.

Bray's long-term friendship with WWE announcer Jojo Offerman after his marriage to Samantha led to rumors that he had an extramarital affair with Jojo. In 2022, the couple got engaged. Jojo announced the two's engagement on Instagram on April 28, 2022.

She wrote: "A million times YES! in a picture showcasing my sparkling ring. Even though it feels like we've been together forever, Windham and I were still in love and engaged to be married at the time of his passing.

Children

Did Bray Wyatt have any kids?
Bray had four different children. With Samantha, he had two kids: Kendyl was born in 2011 and Cadyn was born in 2013.

Following their divorce, Samantha eventually accused Bray of excluding these two kids; it is unknown if he was still in contact with them at the time of his passing.

He had two children with Jojo in addition to Cadyn and Kendyl, even though they were never wed. According to Jojo's Instagram photos, Bray appears to have been a loving father to both of their children, a male named Knash in 2019 and a daughter named Hyrie Von in 2020.

Chapter 7: The Departure

When he was released from his contract in July 2021, Bray Wyatt's WWE career came to an end. Many fans were shocked by the revelation because Wyatt had been one of the company's most well-liked and prosperous performers in recent years.

Wyatt's departure was motivated by several factors. While some fans felt that WWE had underused him, others thought his character had grown boring. Whatever the cause, the company suffered a great loss when Wyatt was let go.

Wyatt has been relatively silent since leaving WWE. He did not make any public declarations regarding his future goals or appear on any other wrestling promotions. There were, however, speculations that he was engaged in new projects, potentially a horror film.

Luke Harper and Brodie Lee, two of Bray Wyatt's closest friends and colleagues, also passed away. Lee passed away in December 2021 after suffering a heart attack, and Harper passed away in December 2020 from idiopathic pulmonary fibrosis. The two deaths struck Wyatt hard, and they contributed to his decision to leave WWE.

Life After WWE: AEW, Hollywood, and More

His abrupt departure from WWE opened up new opportunities for him, like as his foray into All Elite Wrestling (AEW), Hollywood, and other areas.

In AEW, Bray Wyatt makes his eagerly anticipated debut, shocking the wrestling world. He returned to AEW with the ring name Windham, captivating viewers once more with his enigmatic storytelling and character-driven style. He became an instant sensation on the

AEW roster after his entry into the promotion opened up thrilling opportunities and ideal matches.

Bray Wyatt looked into career opportunities outside the squared circle in Hollywood. He entered cinema and television ventures using his magnetic presence and acting skills, expanding his options as an actor. He was an intriguing choice for a variety of entertainment projects because of his distinctive personality and larger-than-life demeanor.

While Bray Wyatt's post-WWE career found prominence in AEW, he also made appearances in the indie wrestling scene, interacting with fans in close quarters and demonstrating his skills in a variety of wrestling promotions. He was able to establish closer personal connections with his devoted following thanks to these appearances.

Beyond wrestling and entertainment, Bray Wyatt was extremely inventive. He experimented with artistic endeavors like writing, producing, and perhaps even venturing into the world of podcasting while interacting with his followers and sharing his knowledge, experiences, and stories.

His Demise

In February 2023, Bray retired from professional wrestling due to an unidentified health issue. We eventually discovered that he had COVID-19, which had aggravated pre-existing heart problems. But just a few days before he passed away, it was revealed that he was nearing a potential WWE comeback.

Sadly, that comeback never materialized. However, several well-known wrestlers talked about the legacy that Bray left behind in the ring as the news of his passing spread.

On Thursday, August 24, 2023, Windham Rotunda passed away at the age of 36, much to the dismay of the entire pro-wrestling fraternity. Fans were baffled by Bray Wyatt's death because he had been out of the WWE since February 2023.

The wrestler was reportedly sleeping at the time, and when his fiancee Jojo Offerman heard his alarm go off an hour later without pausing, she reportedly became concerned. According to the media site, Mr. Wyatt was discovered in his bed blue and not breathing. While her mother was performing CPR, his girlfriend dialed 911, but he was eventually pronounced dead at the hospital.

Months after the wrestler received COVID-19 and experienced heart problems as a result of it, the sad tragedy happened. Several heart problems have plagued Bray Wyatt. He should carry a heart defibrillator, according to the doctor.

The defibrillator was not on Mr. Wyatt when he passed away, and it was later discovered inside his car in the driveway, though it is unknown if it could have saved his life.

Mr. Wyatt had been hospitalized for a cardiac condition a week before passing away. On the morning of his death, he also met with the doctors, who advised him to keep wearing the external defibrillator.

Former WWE wrestler and chief content officer Triple H confirmed Bray Wyatt's passing.

At first, Triple H announced Bray Wyatt's passing via his X (Twitter) account. "Just got a call from WWE Hall of Famer Mike Rotunda who broke the heartbreaking news that our WWE family member for life Windham Rotunda passed away unexpectedly earlier today," Hunter said. We ask that everyone respect his family's privacy at this time as we have them in our thoughts.

Shocked fans flooded Triple H's Twitter with questions and condolences as soon as the news of Bray Wyatt's passing was confirmed. In addition to this, other WWE stars expressed their sorrow over Bray Wyatt's loss on their social media accounts.

Dwyane "The Rock" Johnson, a WWE legend and well-known Hollywood actor, expressed his sorrow over Bray Wyatt's loss. He and the Rotunda family have my undying respect and love. Loved his presence, his ring work, his promos, and his link to the WWE universe. The character is very uncommon, cool, and difficult to build in the wild world of pro wrestling. Still absorbing Terry Funk yesterday and now Bray today after losing the goat...I send the Rotunda family and the Funk family my love, light, strength, and mana during this trying and tragic time.

Bray Wyatt's death reason
Bray Wyatt's cardiac problems were "exacerbated" as a result of getting COVID earlier this year (2023), according to reports of his death from a heart attack. However, neither Rotunda's family nor the police have yet to identify the precise reason for his demise.

Tributes

JoJo Offerman paid homage to her late fiancée, WWE star Bray Wyatt, in a post.
Many celebrities sent condolences to Offerman as well. She shared many images of their family along with a sweet tribute to her fiance on Instagram.

"I've written and rewritten this post so many times because there are no amount of words in this world to describe Windham and what he means to me," Offerman wrote. "But I've also been avoiding it because, in some weird way, it makes all of this all too real. I miss the love of my life so much it hurts. He was everything I ever wanted and everything I never knew I needed, and I let him know that every day."

She claimed that Wyatt was both "the best person I know" and her soul mate. She claimed that he made everyone feel unique and emphasized the importance of family to him, particularly in terms of his role as a father to their children and the two children he had before them.

"I cry because I wish we had more time baby, but I smile because I was so blessed to be loved by you in the time we did have. I will always love you, Windham," she said. "I will always show our kids how incredible their daddy is. I will always make sure they know how much you love them. And I will always make you proud just like you made me proud. I love you forever baby, until we meet again."

Through its live events and performances, WWE and its performers have kept up their remembrance of Wyatt. Additionally, the business is giving Offerman and Bray's kids all net profits from Wyatt merchandise sold on the WWE Shop.

WWE athletes made an emotional gesture as a permanent tribute to Bray Wyatt.
The late Bray Wyatt was honored by the WWE family of stars, including Bruan Strowman,

Shotzi, Karrion Kross, and others, by having tattoos of his firefly logo placed on their bodies.

Other WWE Superstars who were unable to attend Rotunda's tribute ceremony, such as World Heavyweight Champion Seth Rollins, Alexa Bliss, and AEW's Miro, also paid respect to Rotunda individually. His influence extends beyond WWE in the realm of wrestling. During AEW's "All In" pay-per-view, Buddy Matthews carried the firefly lantern as a memorial to Wyatt. The lantern was out, and the only light in the room came from cellphones that resembled the firefly that served as his emblem.

In addition, Premier League team Arsenal honored Wyatt by playing "Broken Out In Love" by Mark Crozer throughout the half of their game against Fulham on August 26, 2023. The final score of the game was 2-2.

WWE sent their sympathies to friends and family.

"WWE is saddened to learn that Windham Rotunda, also known as Bray Wyatt, passed away on Thursday, August 24, at age 36," WWW wrote on X, previously known as Twitter. "WWE extends its condolences to Rotunda's family, friends, and fans."

John Cena expressed his condolences to the deceased's family and said that the death has left him "devastated."

"Devastated by the news of the passing of Windham Rotunda. My heart goes out to the entire Rotunda family," he wrote.

"Windham brought the best out of me in so many ways. I'm forever grateful for the moments we shared. A sad day for all those he reached around the world. RIP."

The Rock said, 'I'm heartbroken by the news of Bray Wyatt's passing. Always had tremendous respect and love for him and the Rotunda family. Loved his presence, promos, in-ring work, and connection with the @wwe universe. Very a unique, cool, and rare character, which is hard to create in our crazy world of pro wrestling. Still processing losing the goat, Terry Funk yesterday, and now Bray today.'

My love, light, strength & mana to the Rotunda family and Funk family during this tough, heartbreaking time, he concluded.

RIP BRAY WYATT. This is awful news, just sad for his family, friends, and fans. I thought so highly of Bray Wyatt and was so flattered when he started using the mandible claw for his finisher. He was a true visionary; one of the most compelling presences that wrestling has ever seen.' Mick Foley wrote.

Titus O'Neil: "Heartbroken is an understatement to my feelings at the moment about this news. Windham was the consummate professional, the Ultimate Teammate, and a Wonderful Father, Husband, Brother, Friend, and son. I and my Family send our Condolences and support"

Sonya Deville: "I'm at a loss for words....I'm grateful to have witnessed his greatness and been around his sweet spirits, always so nice and kind, and willing to help. My prayers to all his family"

Ivar: "This has gutted me. He welcomed us to the main roster with open arms and was so kind to us. I just don't know what to say"

Chelsea Green: "What a horrible loss for his family, his friends, and the entire wrestling world. He was a creative genius and I will forever be influenced by his work."

Natalya: "My heart breaks for Windham and his family. You were always so nice to us, Windham. Ever since we were kids, going trick or treating together, following our dad's footsteps. You were always relatable, kind, and humble. We will always be so grateful for your presence in our lives."

Additionally, WWE released the following statement on Bray Wyatt's merchandise sales on the WWE Shop:

"In the wake of Bray Wyatt's death, WWE will donate all net proceeds to support JoJo Offerman and his children."

IN THE ANNALS OF PROFESSIONAL WRESTLING, FEW PERSONAS HAVE LEFT AS INDELIBLE A MARK AS BRAY WYATT. THE LEGACY CONTINUES; THE

END IS JUST A NEW BEGINNING.

A Heartfelt Tribute to Wrestling's Mysterious Maestro

Certain moments in the realm of professional wrestling leave an indelible mark on the business. Moments that go beyond the fights and plotlines, moments that serve as a reminder of why we fell in love with this extravagant show. I honor Bray Wyatt, one of these individuals who evolved into a dynamic mystery in the squared circle.

I'm sitting down to think about Bray Wyatt's life and I feel as though I'm saying farewell to a great icon as I do so. I know I'm not the only one who feels this way, but the mystique, the darkness, and the unmatched storytelling that Bray brought to WWE will always hold a special place in my heart.

From the moment he uttered those chilling words, "We're here," as the leader of The Wyatt

Family, I was hooked. His ability to captivate, to make us suspend our disbelief, and to immerse us in his world was a testament to his unparalleled talent.

Through it all, I respected Bray Wyatt's relentless commitment to his job. I saw his highs and lows, his title victories, and terrible defeats.

This tribute is not just a farewell; it's a celebration of a truly exceptional performer who impacted our lives and made us believe in the magic of wrestling.

Bray Wyatt, your mystique is eternal, and your legacy will never fade. We are grateful for the stories, chills, and memories that will last a lifetime in our hearts.

Appendix I: Bray Wyatt's Best Quotes

"I'm not a monster. I'm just a man who sees the world for what it is."

"We all have a darkness inside of us. It's up to each of us to decide whether or not we let it consume us."

"The only way to overcome your fear is to face them head-on."

"Don't be afraid to be different. Be afraid to be the same."

"The world is a cruel and unforgiving place. But it's also a beautiful place, full of love and hope. It's up to us to decide which world we want to live in."

"I'm not here to win matches; I'm here to change the world."

"Fear is just a four-letter word."

"In this world of gods and monsters, I am the devil."

"We have entered the bowels of Carcosa, friend. But don't you worry about a thing? I'll make it quick." – Friday Night SmackDown, March 14, 2014

"The world does not have a voice of its own. It can't tell you what it wants, what it needs. But it's yearning for something to point it in the right direction. A savior, perhaps. Save us, Chris! You must forgive me. Where have my manners gone? I don't think I've had a chance to formally introduce myself. You may call me Bray Wyatt. But I have a thousand faces and a million names. Seducer, accuser, destroyer. I am the color red in a world full of black and white, and if you value your ability to breathe… don't get too close. Save us, Chris. Save yourself." – Friday Night SmackDown, March 21, 2014

"John Cena tells all of you that I am a monster, and he is right. I am a monster, and oh how cruel I can be. He would also have you believe that my message, my honorable message, is nothing but lies and that I only wish to watch the world burn. I have to give it to you, John, you're right again. I do wish to watch this world burn. I wish to watch it burn as a farmer watches his spoiled crops burn so they may rise again. This world must be burned down so that it can be reborn. And it will be reborn in my image, the image of Wyatt." – Monday Night Raw, May 5, 2014.

"My soul smiles at just the thought of your quivering hands waving those white flags, yeah. I would advise y'all to be careful inviting the devil in your backyard … because he may just like it and decide to stay." – Friday Night SmackDown, January 31, 2014

"This is where our story ends. I have no mercy left to give. It could have been different, it could have been better, it could have been perfect. But now this is your fault. I am going to punish you.

I want you to open your eyes, open your eyes, and look at your dismay. Open your eyes, Bryan, this is the end." – Monday Night Raw, December 30, 2013

'I'm not afraid of death. I'm not afraid of anything.'

'I don't like to diet. I think it's stupid. You only live once. I do like to train just because of the simple reason that it doesn't hurt as much. I need to keep myself as strong as I can be. That's just who I am as a man, and I think a lot of people have the same idea.'

'I don't need anyone creatively to tell me how I'm supposed to be. Only I know the answer to that. Only I know what I would say. That's always been my outlook. I haven't worried about rubbing people wrong because I only know how to be Bray. And Bray is always going to be Bray.'

' You have to prepare yourself mentally and physically by training and knowing how to take care of yourself the best you can so that you're able to fight and get to where you want to be.'

'I don't think I think things through like regular people would. I could be a hateful person, and I also don't care about my well-being, I guess. I just kind of have that knack about me. I just don't care.'

'I have to sit alone in a room and be alone with my thoughts. It always starts with an idea, and once the idea grows, I have a concept of what I want to say, and once I go out there and start feeling the energy, that concept grows and becomes whatever it is.'

'I think the thing about keeping your character fresh is, when you change as an individual, you have to flow with it.'

'When I say things, when I speak on television, I'm not making stuff up. I'm not, like, sitting in the back with a notepad thinking, 'Maybe this will make them think I'm crazy'. That's how I am, you know? My views on this and that, which I don't want to delve into, but my views are that of the real me. There is no character.'

'School is not for me. I'm volatile and hate being told what to do.'

'There are times when fans don't understand that change is inevitable or that changes are done too fast. They say, 'We like the way you used to be.' Or they say, 'We liked what you did then.' You can't stay the same. As you mature as an adult, you find out you have to keep changing in this business. It's something The Undertaker laid on me.'

' Everyone thinks of me as some weird swamp trash pro wrestler, and that's okay - think what you want - but I'm an intelligent person, and I have my views on the world.'

'Since day one, my inception, when I came into the world - I had my eyes on power. The WWE championship is power.'

'If I was to feel guilty about something, it would be the fact I haven't done enough. I wish there was a million Roman Reigns. So that I could take them all out at once. Then I would feel like I've accomplished something.'

'I am a well-spoken, educated person, and I'm also an extremely accomplished athlete. For me, it's disrespect and a slap in the face when people say I broke a mold as champion or I don't fit as champion.'

'Once upon a time, I liked to call myself 'The Grandfather of NXT' because I was one of the first to come up as I was, from NXT.'

'The first time I fought Undertaker. I remember watching him walk down and having this chill. You know that feeling when you're almost getting into a car accident? It felt like that continuously for 10 minutes. That was a moment.'

'That generic outlook of what a 'WWE champion' should be is a joke to me. The casual fan walks in and expects to see a guy in short trunks with abs and a shaven body. I do not believe in that.'

'Vince McMahon is not a human being. They don't make people like Vince. Vince is Vince. I can't even describe to you what it's like being in a room with Vince McMahon. He is above man. That's the best way I can put it. Like-minded people take over the world, so I've always had a great rapport with him.'

'When you watch 'UFC,' there is not a cliche champion who looks the same every time.'

'When you go into a 'WWE' ring, you know you're going to compete. You know that things are going to hurt. It is a dangerous, dangerous place. No matter what people think or say, it's a very, very dangerous thing.'

'John Cena is the man here. He's the Hulk Hogan of our era.'

'The first time you go out and perform at WrestleMania, it's a very challenging thing. It's the showcase of immortals, and you don't know what to expect, and every WrestleMania is different.'

'If I were Goldberg or Brock Lesnar, I wouldn't want to have to go on after me and Randy. From their standpoint, I wouldn't want to be them and have to go on after us.'

'When you go out there, and you're in the ring, honestly, half the time you forget what city you're even in because you're so focused on what you're doing and the task at hand.'

Appendix II: Bray Wyatt's Best Promos

1. Debut Promo
2. The Firefly Fun House
3. The "Sister Abigail" Tease
4. Feud with John Cena
5. Promos as "The Fiend"
6. Promo Before WrestleMania 37
7. "The Man in the Woods"
8. Promo on Daniel Bryan's Transformation
9. Promo on Braun Strowman
10. Promo with John Cena at WrestleMania 36
11. "Abandon All Hope" Promo
12. Promo on The Undertaker
13. Promo on Finn Bálor
14. Promo on Seth Rollins
15. Promos as "The Cult Leader"
16. Promo on Roman Reigns
17. Promo during the "Compound Fight" with Matt Hardy

18. "Firefly Fun House" Mockery of John Cena Promo on Daniel Bryan's Return
19. Promo on Randy Orton's Betrayal

Appendix III: Bray Wyatt's Discography-Theme Music and Entrance Themes

"Live in Fear" (The Wyatt Family)
"Broken Out in Love" (The Wyatt Family)
"The Whole World in His Hands" (The Wyatt Family)
"Live in Fear" (Solo)
"Let Me In" (The Fiend)
"Heal" (The Fiend)
"Voices" (Temporary)

Made in the USA
Monee, IL
12 November 2023

46389436R00039